ABSOLUTE BEGINNERS

Flute

To acces audio visit:
www.halleonardmgb.com/mylibrary
Enter Code
5012-6923-9897-1943

Hal•Leonard®

Published by
Hal Leonard

Exclusive Distributors:
Hal Leonard
7777 West Bluemound Road
Milwaukee, WI 53213
Email: info@halleonard.com

Hal Leonard Europe Limited
42 Wigmore Street
Marylebone, London, W1U 2RY
Email: info@halleonardeurope.com

Hal Leonard Australia Pty. Ltd.
4 Lentara Court
Cheltenham, Victoria, 3192 Australia
Email: info@halleonard.com.au

Order No. AM1002419
ISBN 9781849389174
This book © Copyright 2011 Hal Leonard

Written by Ned Bennett
Edited by Lizzie Moore
Book design by Chloë Alexander
Photography by Matthew Ward
Models: Danielle Jałowiecka and Gareth Hanson
Audio performance and technical advice: Alison Hayhurst
Backing tracks arranged and produced by Ned Bennett

www.halleonard.com

Contents

Introduction

One of the oldest instruments known to man, flutes have been discovered dating from prehistoric times. Ever since, examples carved out of bone, bamboo or wood have been played as part of the native culture of many countries around the world, including India, China, Peru and Australia. Most classical musicians use a modern metal instrument, which is based on a flute designed by Theobald Boehm in 1830.

The flute is a vital part of any orchestra with repertoire ranging from Abel to Zemlinsky, and there is a huge amount of solo and chamber music on offer to any flautist. For good measure, the flute is equally at home in concert bands, military bands, funk bands, folk bands, and bands that play music from India, Ireland, China, Japan, Kazakhstan, Peru, in fact almost anywhere on the planet.

In choosing to play the flute, you will have access to just about the widest range of musical experience possible. And this book is here to start you off.

Easy-to-follow instructions will guide you through:

- How to practise

- Assembling and looking after your flute

- Playing your first notes

- Reading music

- Developing your tone and musical confidence

- Playing your first pieces

No proper musical instrument plays itself and nobody has yet invented a magic wand that will instantly turn you into an expert flautist, so the only way to improve is practice.

15 to 20 minutes every day is far better than two hours at the weekend. Most of what we learn, we forget soon after. Frequent practice sessions that follow a routine will help you to develop muscle memory, which is when certain actions like breathing, mouth shape and finger combinations become automatic.

Repetition

Playing an instrument is a combination of around 80% mechanical action and 20% mental exercise. The more times you repeat a mechanical action, the more automatic it will become. Music happens at set speeds, which means that you will often not have time to think of what your hands or your mouth are doing. The frustrating thing is, just when you think you have mastered a mechanical action, you will then forget it overnight. That is why it is essential to practise the same material for several days in a row. Each time you will forget a little less until the action is firmly lodged in your long-term memory.

Patience

The more patience you have, the quicker you will improve. Make sure one particular point is properly internalised before you move on to the next. Trying to do too much too early will leave gaps in your playing that will hinder you at a later point. After all, learning the flute is not a race.

The online audio that comes with this book is designed to encourage you to practise. Some of the backing tracks are quite long, as they incorporate many repetitions of new finger combinations or tone production exercises. Use these backing tracks every time you play as they will help pace your practice sessions.

What's in the case?

The flute is made up of three sections: the headjoint, the body, and the footjoint. Student flutes are made from an alloy of copper, zinc and nickel. This is then plated in either nickel or silver. More expensive flutes are made from solid silver or even gold!

Most flutes have solid keys for the fingers that make them easy to cover, but some have small holes in the middle of the keys which more advanced players may prefer.

Your flute kit should also include the following:

* A gauze or swab with which to clear away the moisture each time after you play

* A wooden rod to push the cloth through the flute

* A case

* A soft cleaning cloth for wiping the outside of the flute

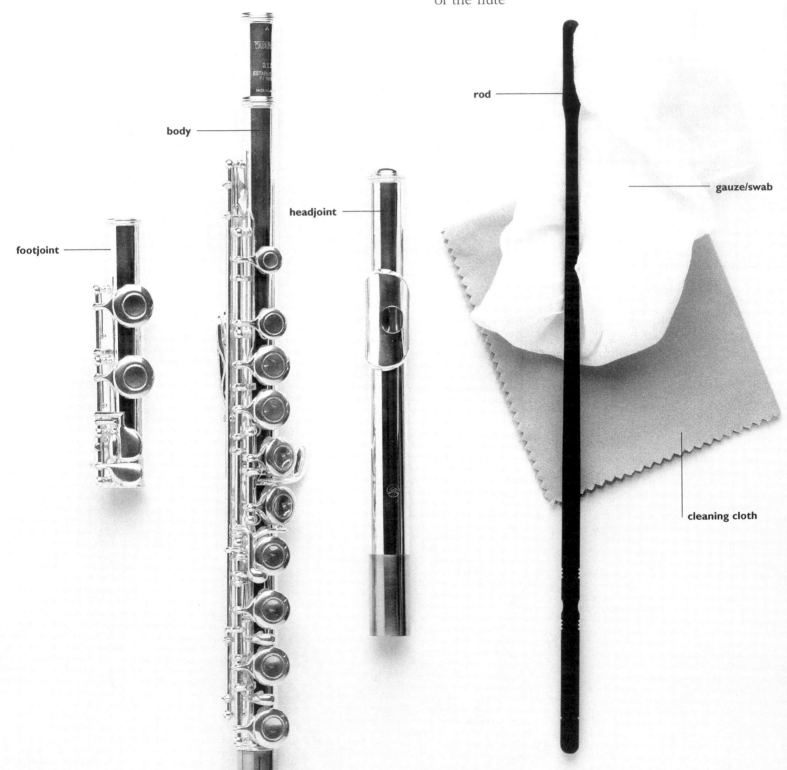

body

footjoint

headjoint

rod

gauze/swab

cleaning cloth

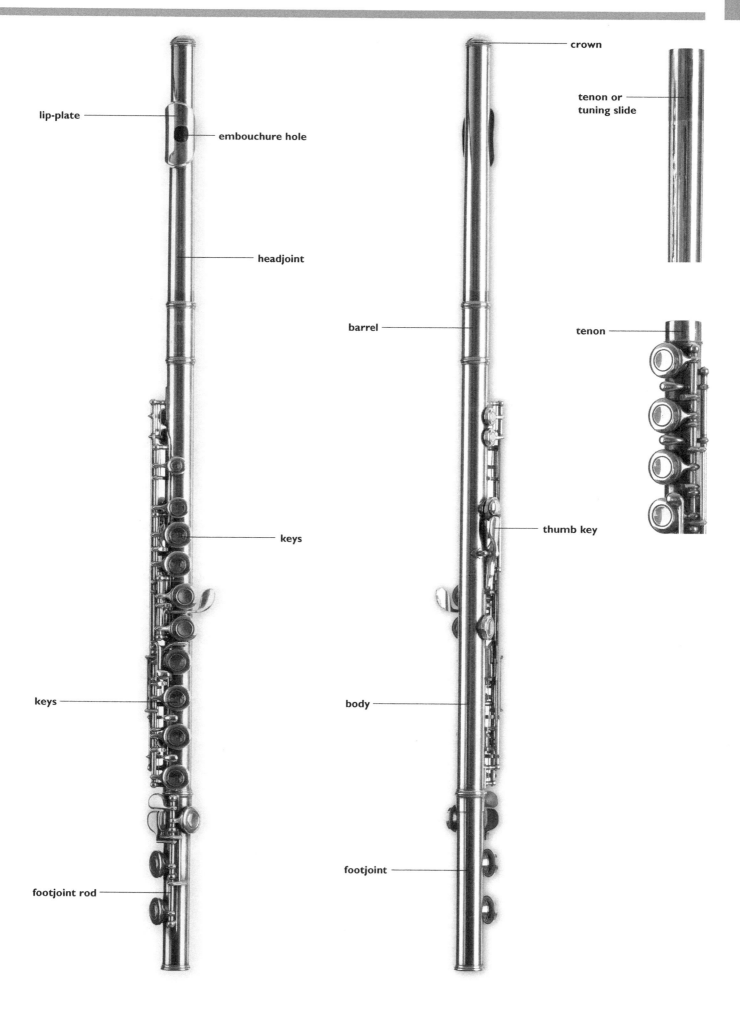

lip-plate

embouchure hole

headjoint

keys

keys

footjoint rod

crown

tenon or tuning slide

barrel

tenon

thumb key

body

footjoint

Taking care of your flute

A flute is an expensive and precisely engineered instrument, so it is very important to look after it.

NEVER use any kind of polish or grease on your flute. It will spoil the plating and interfere with the mechanics. Also, **NEVER** oil your flute yourself. That is a job for a skilled and experienced repairer. Do use a soft *microfibre* cloth to carefully wipe off fingerprints, but only where you have easy access to the metal. Don't try to insert a cloth between keys or under rods.

IMPORTANT
Do not keep the swab inside your flute case with the flute: it would be the same as not having dried it at all!

Using the swab and cleaning rod
The full routine of cleaning your flute will be explained later on, but you can prepare for it at this point.

Every time you finish playing, the inside of your flute will be wet with condensation. Moisture is bad for the pads (the white discs under the keys), and will also tarnish the metal.

You must clean this moisture away with your swab.

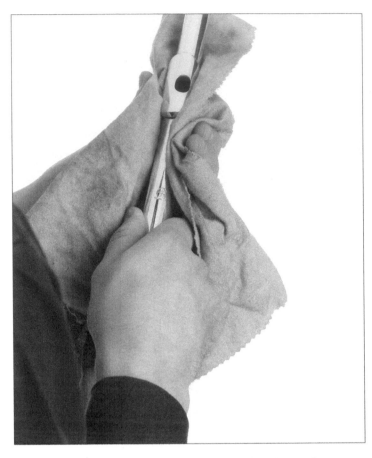

Push a corner of the swab through the slit at the top of the cleaning rod. Feed it through a few inches, lift it over the top and then wrap it round, so no part of the rod could be exposed to scratch the inside of the flute. This strange artistic creation is what you will use to dry the inside of your flute.

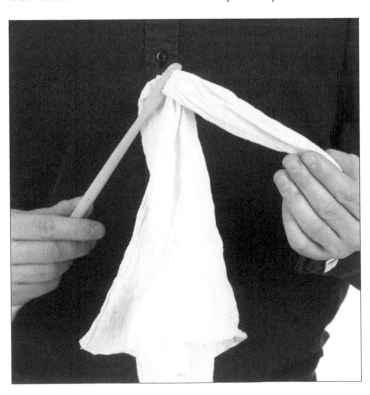

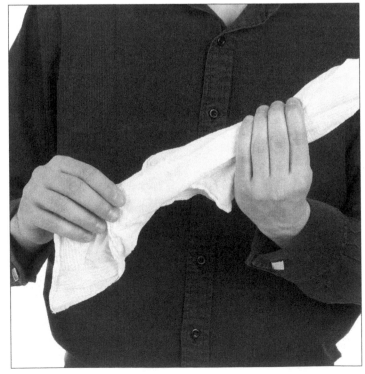

This is something we all do thousands of times every day, although we never really give any thought to it. When playing the flute, however, you need to breathe in a certain way to be in control of the sound and to not cause you to feel uncomfortable.

Open throat
Find a mirror or a window and steam it up by blowing on it. Not all in one big rush, but slowly so you cover as wide an area as you can. When you do this, your throat will be more open than in its usual relaxed state. (The air feels warmer and isn't sped up by being forced through a small hole.) Now try breathing in quickly with the same throat shape. This should feel a bit like gasping and you will feel a cold spot at the back of your throat. You should try to breathe in and out in the ways described here when you play the flute.

Using your diaphragm
Now try to find a drinking straw. Place it between your lips and breathe out. Now try to force the air out more quickly. As you do this you should feel the muscles around your stomach tighten a bit. These muscles control the diaphragm, the large, flat membrane that forms the bottom of your lung cavity.

As you breathe in and out you must use your diaphragm.

You will have so much more control over your breathing than if you lift your shoulders to breathe.

Keep your shoulders down!

Embouchure and your first sounds

Embouchure is the posh word that means *'the shape of your mouth when playing a woodwind or brass instrument'*.

Be prepared to read through and carry out all the tasks on these pages a number of times. Just because you may be lucky and get a good sound straight away, it does not mean you will be able to do so every time, and *every time* is what counts.

1 With your best French accent, say the word 'tu', as in 'tu es belle'. The hole that your lips form should be very small. You should feel your bottom jaw move slightly forwards, and your lips are pulled very slightly sideways.

2 Now breathe in with an open throat (a slow gasp), and say 'tu' again, this time without engaging your vocal cord. Try this a few times as it will need to be automatic.

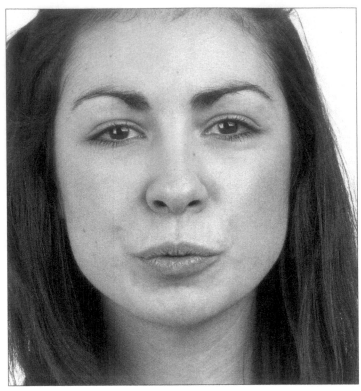

3 Lift the headjoint out of the case carefully by its ends. For this section you will not need the rest of the flute.

4 Holding the headjoint with the open end to your right and the embouchure hole on top, pull it in towards you, so that the edge of the embouchure hole ends up on the bottom edge of your lower lip, and the lip-plate nestles just above the natural curve of your chin. Look in a mirror if it helps, though you should be able to feel it too.

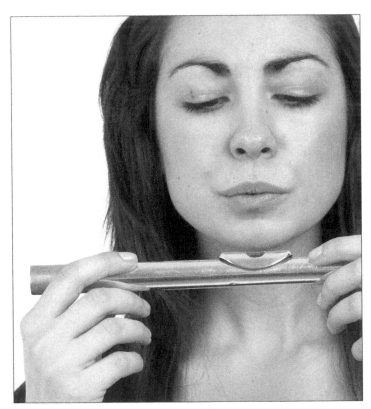

5 Try playing a note. Breathe in (open throat). Then, with your best embouchure, (the 'u' as in 'tu') blow across the hole, not too hard, but more than just your normal breath.

Keep your cheeks flat, and don't blow downwards *into* the hole. The air should be directed *across the top* of the embouchure hole. Try this a few times until you produce a note each time.

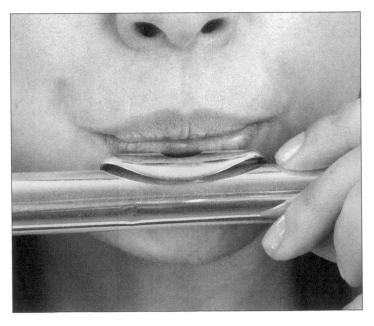

Roll the headjoint towards you, then away from you, trying to play a note as you go. At some point you may find the sound dramatically improves. You should listen to the pitch of this note.

As you roll the headjoint away from you, the pitch will go up little by little until the sound disappears completely. The best tone is usually achieved when the pitch is almost but not entirely as high as it will go.

At this point you may feel the whole headjoint resonates in your fingers! Once you have found this point, practise removing the headjoint from your mouth, pausing, replacing it and playing a note. You need to practise finding this position automatically every time you play.

Getting the sound

If you did not manage to produce a note, don't worry. There are many adjustments that can be made to help. If you did play a note, then try all the following points anyway to improve your sound.

Do these actions slowly taking a good rest between each attempted note otherwise you may hyperventilate.

Check that the near *edge* of the embouchure hole is in contact with the bottom edge of your lower lip, right in line with the opening between your lips where the air emerges. (A mirror will help here as it might not be quite central.)

Try raising and lowering the headjoint. Even an adjustment of a millimetre can make a difference.

Now try *tonguing* the notes. Just as in saying 'tu', your tongue starts off by touching the roof of your mouth just above your teeth. The air pressure builds up, then is released cleanly by gently letting go with the tongue.

Listen to **Track 1** where you will hear a professional flautist experimenting with rolling the headjoint. You will hear her search for the best sound and then play several *tongued* notes with everything in the correct position.

Towards the end, play along to see if your best note is in tune with hers.

Assembling the flute

Although there are only three sections to the flute, care must be taken when putting it together in order not to damage any of the moving parts.

Stand or sit with the case open on a table in front of you.

1 Carefully, *without pulling any rods or keys*, lift the body of the flute out by the edge near the barrel. When it is clear of the case, put the fingers of your left hand around the barrel avoiding contact with any keys or rods. You should have a firm hold, but not a tight grip.

2 With your right hand take the footjoint out of the case by its edge. Hold it as close to the foot as possible with your thumb *lightly* pressing the lowest key to give you some control. Bring it round to the tenon at the foot of the body and gently twist it into place. *Never waggle or push the tenon into the footjoint as you may damage your flute*.

3 Again with care, lift out the headjoint and hold it lightly around the middle. Making sure it is *dead straight* in relation to the main body, very gently twist the tenon of the headjoint all the way into the barrel. When it is fully in, twist it back out just a few millimetres. This is how you will tune your flute later on.

Aligning the parts

The final stage of assembly is to line up the parts of the flute. First, align the embouchure hole with the keys on the top of the flute.

Next, align the long rod on the footjoint with the centre of the very bottom key on the body.

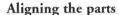

Now that your flute is assembled you can hold it lightly in either hand, but remember never to squeeze tightly or you may damage it. The next step is to get the hands into the correct position in order to play.

1 Place the top joint of your left thumb over the paddle-shaped key on the underside of the flute. More than just the tip should be protruding above the key.

2 The fingers of your left hand curl around the flute with the lowest section of your index finger pressing firmly against the body, a bit more towards the barrel than your thumb. Press down lightly on the keys as shown.

Your fingers should be able to cover the middle of each of these keys and will be pointing away from you when you play.

Don't try to make your fingers approach the flute at 90 degrees.

3 Place the tip of your right thumb on the underside of the flute directly underneath the third key from the foot end of the body. Curl your fingers and without pressing down, cover the lowest three keys on the body.

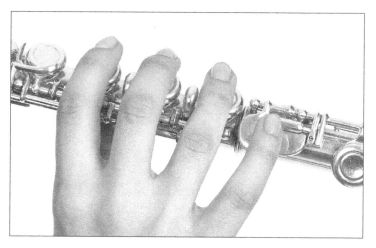

4 Press the very top key on the footjoint with your right little finger. Unlike most of the keys, this one will stay pressed down most of the time that you are playing.

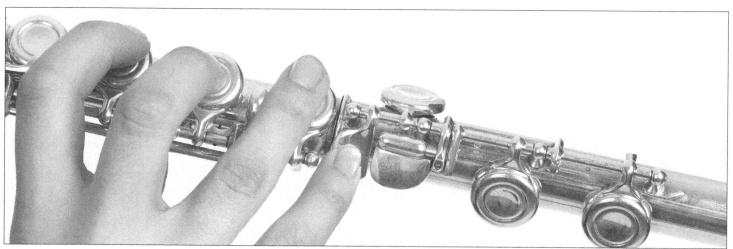

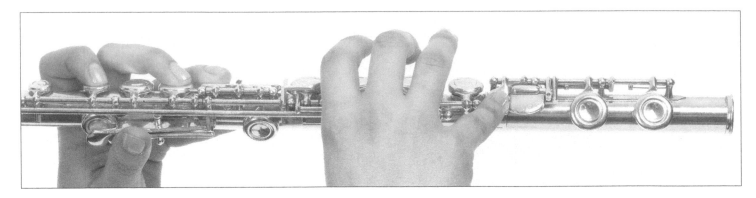

14 The note **G**

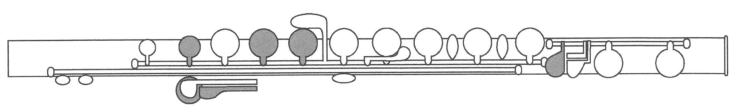

Listen to **Track 2** to hear what the note G should sound like.

The ability to read music is very important to speed up your learning of the flute.

Each note is written down as a 'dot' on a group of five lines called a stave. The stave is like a musical ladder: the higher up the stave a dot is, the higher the note. G is fairly low and appears on the 2nd line up from the bottom of the stave.

Playing the note G

Finger the note as shown above, using three fingers and the thumb of your left hand, and your right little finger. Lift the flute up in front of you, not quite at arms length, but so that you can see the whole instrument, and with the lip plate in front of your mouth. The flute should slope slightly down to the right as you look at it. Pull the whole flute in towards you so that the edge of the embouchure hole ends up in contact with the bottom edge of your lower lip, bang in front of your blowing aperture. The lip-plate nestles just above the natural curve of your chin.

Always bring the flute in towards you, not upwards from below.

With the lip-plate firmly pulled in to place, (just as you did with the headjoint alone), use the techniques described in the previous pages to play the note **G** a few times so that it comes out reliably. Take your time and relax between every attempt. If the sound is not quite right, or if there is no note at all, check the following:

- Did you breathe with an open throat? (see page 9)

- Is your embouchure correct? Are you thinking '*tu*'? (see page 10)

- Is the embouchure hole in front of your blowing aperture? (see page 11)

- Is the headjoint aligned properly with the body of the flute? (see page 12)

- Try rolling the flute towards or away from you slightly. (see page 11)

- Are you pushing keys that you shouldn't?

If you are struggling, carefully remove the headjoint twisting it out of the body. Retrace your steps through pages 10 and 11. You must not feel disappointed if you have to do this. Playing a note with the flute assembled is very different to playing with just the headjoint alone.

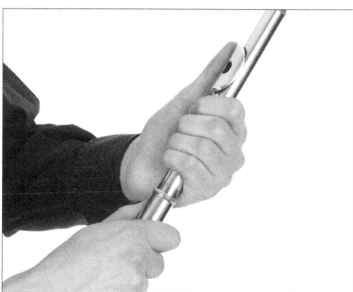

Counting

To play music, not only must you play the correct notes, but you must also play those notes for the correct amount of time. This means you must count when you play.

Music is counted in *beats*. Listen to **Track 3** which is counted in groups (or *bars*) of four beats.

The start of each bar is shown by a *barline*. Follow the music printed below. You will hear a *count-in* of four beats, then the note **G** played for four beats. Next is a rest for four beats, then another note and so on. In total you will hear eight notes.

Now play this piece for yourself using **Track 4** as a backing.

The note **A**

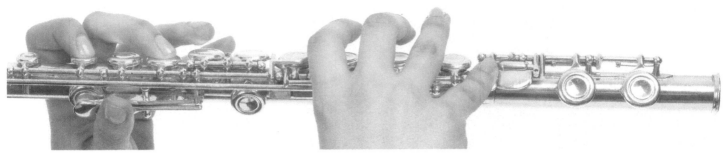

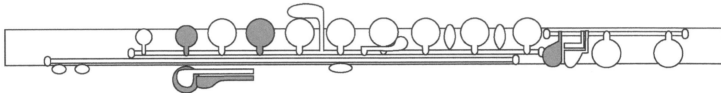

A is written in the second space up from the bottom of the stave.

For the note **A** you need just two fingers of your left hand as well as the thumb, and don't forget the right little finger. Listen to **Track 5** to hear how this note should sound.

Now play the following exercise using **Track 6** as a backing. Look carefully and you will notice that the note changes at some point!

Different note lengths

Notes that last for four beats are called *semibreves* and look like an *oval* placed somewhere on the stave. Notes that last for just two beats are called *minims*. They look the same but have a stem pointing either up or down.

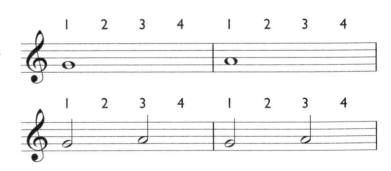

Listen to **Track 7**. This exercise contains semibreves and minims as well as the notes **G** and **A**. Then try to play it using **Track 8** as a backing. Remember to tongue every note and breathe during the rests.

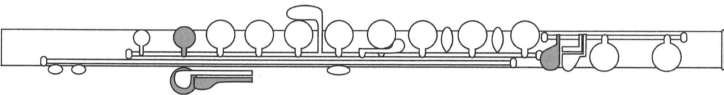

 B is written on the middle line of the stave.

For the note **B** you need just the index finger and thumb of your left hand, and of course your right little finger. On **Track 9** you will hear a B with which you can compare your own.

One more note length

A note that lasts for just one beat is called a *crotchet*.

It looks like a minim but the oval is filled in.
In pieces of music it is very rare that you have to play all the time. For this reason there is a rest for every note length, where you still have to count, but you don't play. Take the opportunity to breathe, or relax if

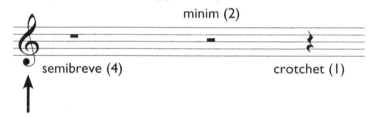

Treble clef you don't need to know much about this yet, but it will appear at the start of every line of flute music.

Try to play this piece before you listen to the demonstration track. It contains everything that you should have learnt so far.

Your backing is on **Track 10** and the demo is on **Track 11**.

Ride With The Tide

Ending your practice session

So you've had enough for the day? I don't blame you. To begin with, practice sessions of 15 to 20 minutes are perfect. If you go on too long your mouth will probably start to ache and you might feel your arms start to hurt.

When you have finished, follow these steps.

1 Wrap the cleaning rod in the swab as described on page 8. Holding the flute by the barrel, insert it up the footjoint, into the flute as far as it will go.

2 With the rod still inserted, untwist the footjoint from the body and put it safely away in the case.

3 Now push the swab further up so that it cleans the whole of the body. Pull the swab back out, untwist the body from the headjoint and put it away.

4 Finally, use the swab to clean the headjoint. You may also choose to clean away fingerprints with your soft cloth, as long as you are careful to avoid damaging any keys.

Congratulations on completing your practice session. Make sure that your next one is very soon. You should then revise all you have done so far. Only when you have understood everything, and can play all the pieces up to this point perfectly, should you choose to continue on into the book.

Be patient, and be honest! Nobody will get everything perfect first time.

The note **C** and tuning up

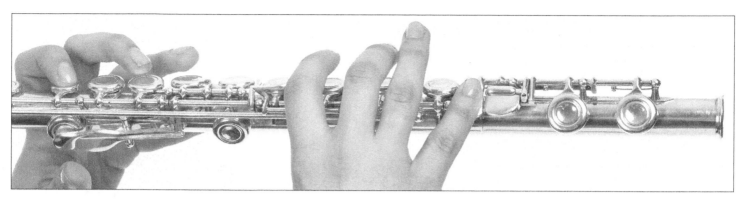

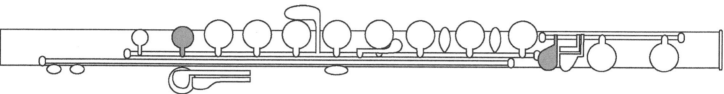

For the note **C** you need just the index finger of your left hand (no thumb), and of course your right little finger. Compare your C with the one on **Track 12**.

C is written in the space just above the middle line of the stave.

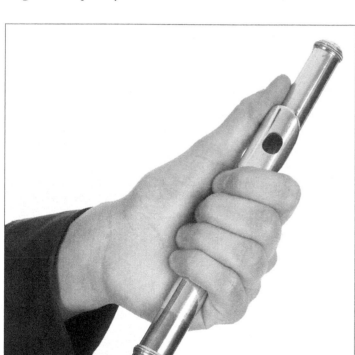

If five flute players were in a room together and all played their note **A** together, more likely than not it would result in a horrible din.

The fact is that tiny differences in embouchure, or in the flute, or the temperature of the instrument will mean that everyone's A will have a slightly different pitch. So when playing with other people or a backing track, you will need to tune up.

1 Make sure your flute is *warmed up*. As you blow warm air across the flute, its temperature will gradually rise. After a minute or so of warming up it should be at the correct pitch.

2 Listen to **Track 13** where you will hear the note A being played continuously. Start playing along, and try to identify if your **A** is *lower* or *higher* than the tuning note **A**.

3 If your note is *lower* than the tuning note, twist your headjoint ***in*** a fraction. If your note is *higher*, twist it ***out***. Try playing along again. Keep adjusting until you are satisfied that you are in tune with the tuning note.

A new note length

Now that you are properly in tune with the tuning note, here is a piece that will give you plenty of practice in counting, recognising notes, tonguing, improving your tone and keeping up with the accompaniment.

First you need to know a new note length.

A dot placed to the right of a note means it is extended or lengthened by half its value. A *minim* lasts for **two beats**. Half its value is **one beat**. So a dotted minim is worth 2+1= **three beats**.

There are four sections to this piece. Each section starts and finishes with a *double barline* with two dots. This instructs you to **repeat** each section, in other words play each section twice.

Breathe during the rests, but don't forget to count! Listen to the demonstration on **Track 14**, practise each section, then play along with **Track 15**.

French Dance

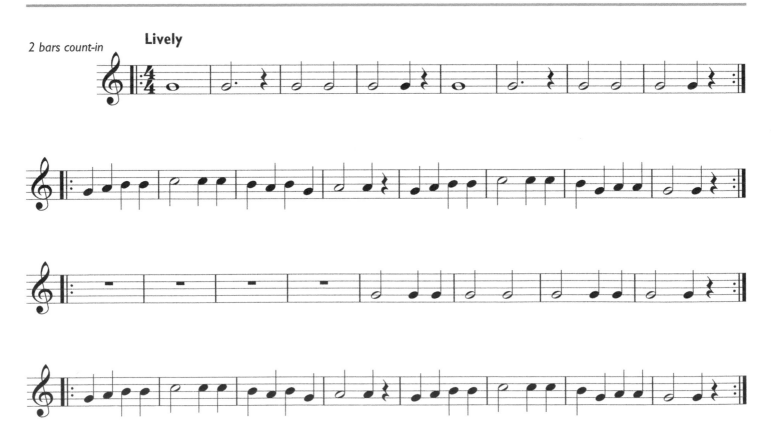

2 bars count-in

Lively

ABSOLUTE BEGINNERS
Flute Fingering Chart

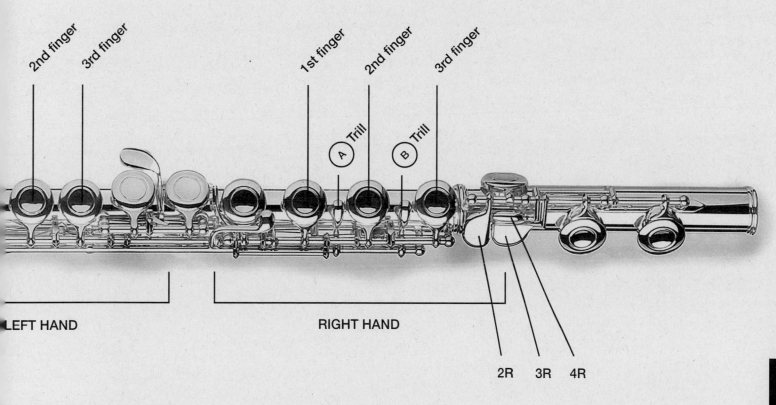

2nd finger

3rd finger

1st finger

2nd finger

3rd finger

A Trill

B Trill

LEFT HAND

RIGHT HAND

2R   3R   4R

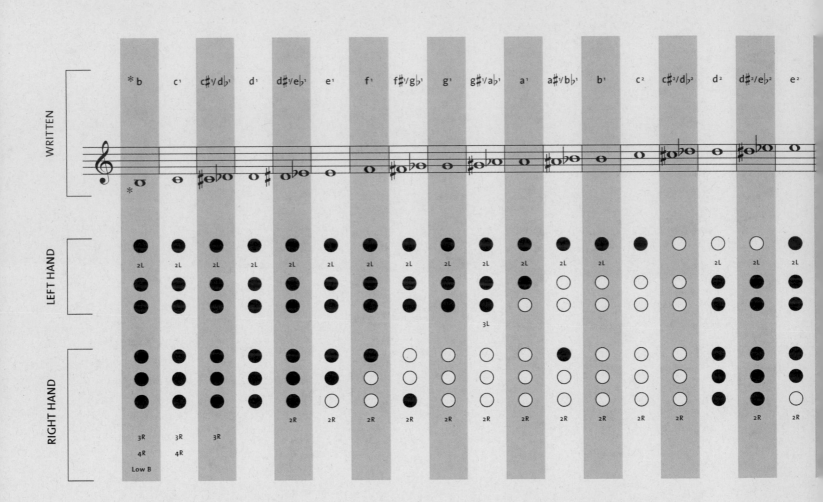

*This note can only be played on flutes with a low B key

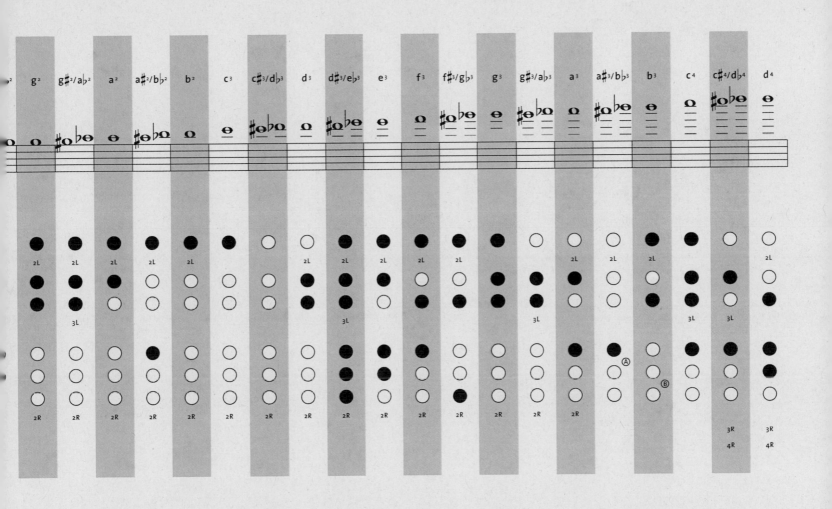

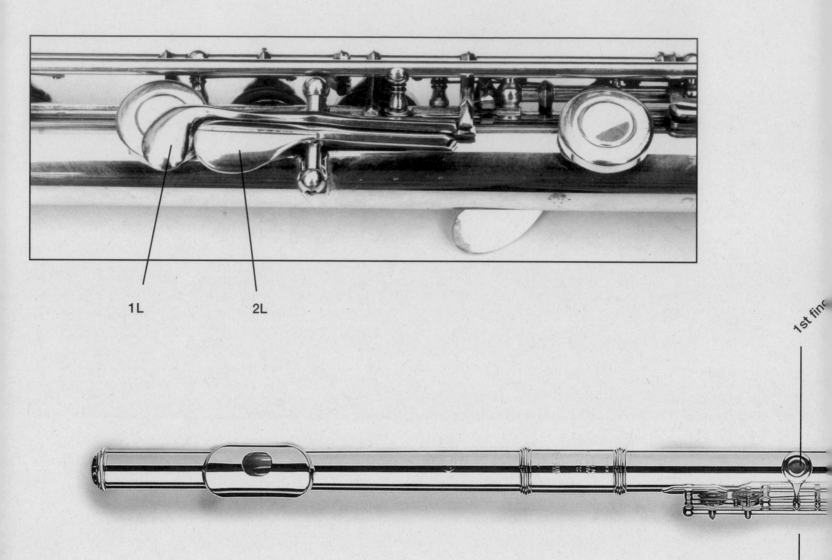

1L   2L

1st fin

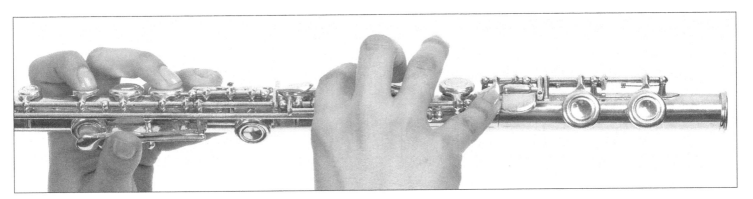

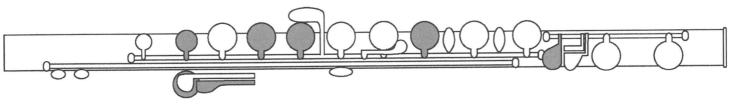

You need three fingers and thumb of your left hand together with your index and little finger of your right hand. You can hear how this note should sound on **Track 16**.

Up to now, apart from your very first sounds, you should have been tonguing every note. This means that all notes are started with the release of the tongue from the roof of the mouth, just behind your top teeth. However, music can seem a bit lumpy if every note is tongued. For this reason, some notes should be *slurred*.

A **slur** is shown by a curved line above or below the notes. Tongue the first note, then simply change the fingering for the other notes in the slur.

F is written in the bottom space of the stave.

In this case, you would tongue the G, then after two beats you would add the first finger in your right hand for the F. The breathing is unaltered and the tongue stays out of the way until needed again.

Listen to the following music on **Track 17**. Notice that it sounds smoother than if all the notes were tongued. This smooth style of playing is called *legato*. Once you have listened to it, play it yourself a few times. Use **Track 18** as a backing.

Slowly

1 bar piano intro

Counting in three

So far all of your pieces and exercises have been counted in groups of four beats, in other words four beats per bar. The following piece is counted in three, just like a waltz. Wait for the two bars of introduction then play. You will need to breathe quickly and

deeply, so make sure your throat is open. Play the slurs as written and make this piece really flow. You will have to practise it a few times before you can play along with the audio as the speed or *tempo* is quite quick.

Skating at Night

Track 19 (demo) **Track 20** (backing)

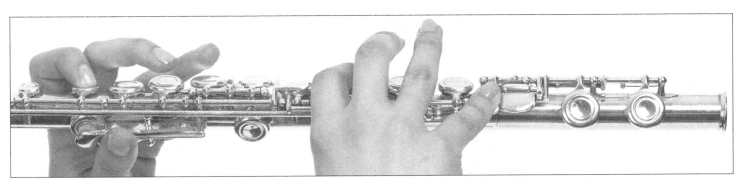

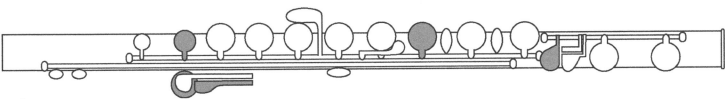

The flat symbol ♭ placed just before a note lowers it by a semitone, the smallest change in pitch that is possible on most instruments. This means that B♭ is lower than B, but not as low as A. There are several ways of playing B♭. Here is the simplest: you need the index fingers of both hands, plus your left thumb and right little finger as usual.

On **Track 21** you will hear a B, then a B♭, and finally an A. Listen to how close together they sound in pitch. Play the three notes yourself. Remember to keep down your right little finger, and don't forget to remove your right index finger for the A.

Here is a waltz with plenty of practice playing B♭s. First try to work out in your head how the rhythm goes. Then practise the notes, phrase by phrase.

When you think you have it, play the whole piece with the backing on **Track 22**.
Finally listen to the performance on **Track 23**.

Waltz in B♭

Expression

Music without expression is like food without flavour, or a garden with no plants. It serves its purpose, but no one would really want it.

You have learnt that slurring notes can make a piece sound smooth (legato), which is ideal for a lullaby, or for faster pieces where lots of rapid tonguing could be too 'lumpy'. Legato playing is a form of expression: the way you play the piece is just as important as the correct notes and rhythms.

Dynamics

One of the easiest ways to make music expressive is to add dynamics. This means making the music loud or quiet by increasing or decreasing the speed of your breath, sometimes with immediate effect or sometimes gradually.

Learn these symbols. They will appear in just about every piece of music that you play.

Symbol	Expression	Meaning
f	*forte*	loud
mf	*mezzo forte*	fairly loud
mp	*mezzo piano*	fairly soft
p	*piano*	soft
<	*crescendo*	gradually get louder
>	*diminuendo*	gradually get softer

The following piece has many expressions. Be sure to follow the dynamics as printed under the music. At the beginning there is an Italian word hinting at the character of the piece. There are slurs to play, and the word *rallentando* near the end tells you to slow down.

The symbol over the last note is called a *pause*. Hold the note on for longer than the four beats.

African Sunset

Track 24 (demonstration) **Track 25** (backing)

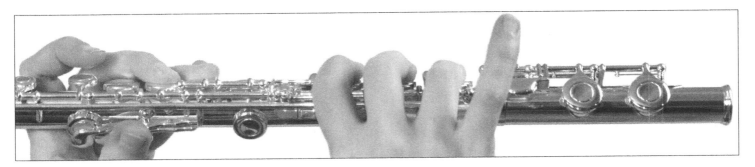

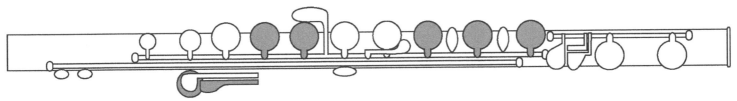

This note is the only one covered in this book where your *right little finger must **not** be pressed down*.

Look at the picture and diagram above to see the correct fingering for this note.

To get the note to sound correctly, tighten your embouchure a fraction to make the hole between your lips a touch smaller, but without pulling the sides of your mouth out into a smile. Increase the airspeed across the embouchure hole (in other words

blow a little harder), and direct the air just a little upwards to get a clean sound. You will hear a D on **Track 26**.

Exercising the little finger

It will probably take much mental wrestling at first to control your right little finger. Below is an exercise that you can play with a backing track, that will help develop a degree of muscle memory. Play this piece every time you practise over a number of days and you will find the finger, breathing and embouchure adjustments become automatic. They will need to in order for you to progress.

Track 27 (backing)

Muscle Memory Madness

Tied notes

You have seen how notes can be one, two, three or four beats in length, however, they can be even longer. Drawing a curved line above or below two notes of the same pitch will tie them together. Here are a couple of examples.

How do we know these aren't just slurs? Easy: slurs will always be drawn over notes of different pitch. For a tie, both notes must be the same pitch.

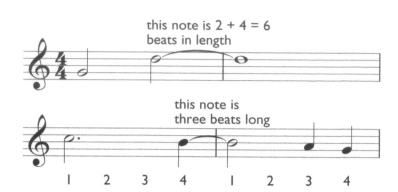

The following piece is marked *Andante con moto* which means literally 'at a walking pace, with movement'. The character is generally calm, but as this is in the style of the early Romantic composers,

you must play the dynamics to turn this into an expressive piece. Breathe properly and deeply to ensure you have enough air for the longer phrases.

Nocturne

Track 28 (backing) **Track 29** (demo)

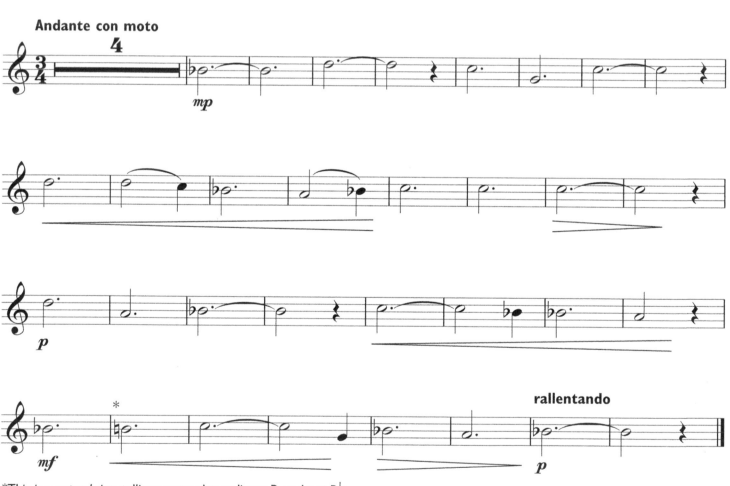

*This is a *natural* sign, telling you to play ordinary B, and not B♭

Whatever instrument you may be studying, it is important to listen to how it should be done properly. Something really made you want to study the flute, or you would not be reading this right now.

So here are a few listening suggestions, just to remind you how amazing great flute playing can be.

- **Bach** *Orchestral Suite no. 2 in B minor*
The flute is featured in this Baroque masterpiece written between 1729 and 1736. The highlight is the energetic last movement, entitled Badinerie.

- **Mozart** *Concerto for Flute no. 1 in G, K313*
A great example of the Classical concerto, written in 1777. The agility of the flute is really exploited in this piece, although there is no shortage of beautiful melody.

- **Debussy** *Syrinx for solo flute*
Written in 1913, this is a beautifully haunting piece with no accompaniment. This type of music is sometimes thought of as equivalent to works by the French Impressionist painters.

- **Hariprasad Chaurasia**
Born in 1938, this astounding Indian musician is a master improviser and performer on the bamboo flute, or *bansuri*. Any of his recordings are worthy of listening, especially of Indian classical music, (Ragas).

- **Paddy Carty**
A true folk flautist from County Galway in the west of Ireland. Playing an unsophisticated *Radcliffe system* flute, he was nevertheless technically highly skilled with a beautifully warm tone. His recordings display great musicality.

- **Jazz flute**
Yes, it does exist, though not enough of it. Listen to Hubert Laws, Herbie Mann, Finn Peters or the occasional moments of Frank Wess in the Count Basie orchestra.

- **Avant Garde**
If you want weird, there are plenty of modern flautists out there who will satisfy your appetite. Listen to Robert Dick in particular who can make the flute do all manner of extraordinary things!

The note E

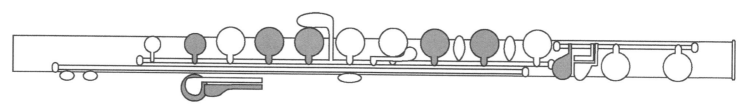

 For this note you need three fingers and thumb of your left hand, and two fingers and the *little finger of your right hand*.

Whereas **D** will always sound correctly, **E** might sound an *octave* (eight notes) too low if you don't adjust your embouchure and airspeed. Check this note against the **E** on **Track 30**.

The middle register

The note **D** (page 25) and this note **E** are in the middle register of the flute. The other notes that you know so far (**G**, **A**, **B**, **B♭** and **C**) are all in the low register. There is a high register, but that is saved for a more advanced book. Middle register notes need:

• A slightly tighter embouchure (smaller hole)

• An upward slant of the airstream (set your bottom lip a tiny bit more forward)

• A faster airspeed

Playing **E** straight off can be a bit tricky. The following exercise may help you to get used to these middle register notes.

The little o symbol above all the **D**s are to remind you to take off your right little finger. Remember to put it back on *all* the other notes. (The os are not normal music notation. You will only see them here, just this once.)

Es with Ease

Track 31 (backing)

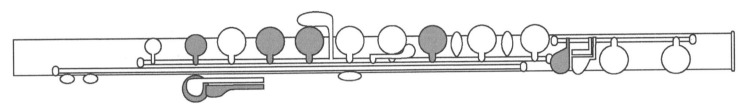

Finger this higher **F** exactly the same as you did for the low **F** (page 21), but change your embouchure and airspeed to make it sound properly. (See how on page 28.)

On **Track 32** you will hear this F, then the low F, then this one once more and so on. These two notes are an *octave* apart. Now you must try to do the same thing, several times over. Your fingers do not move, only your embouchure and airspeed should change.

Musicians use scales to practise many aspects of their playing. There is nothing better to play over and over again to develop tone, breath control, knowledge of notes, smoothness, and just about everything else that needs developing. Here is a scale of **F** *major*.
You will need all the notes that you know from low **F** to high **F**, with **B♭** instead of **B**.

Alternative B♭ fingering

There is a very useful alternative fingering for **B♭** that you can use here. Drag your left thumb to the left so that it now covers the smaller key. *Keep it here for the entire scale except when you have to release it for the note C.* You will now not need your right index finger

for the **B♭**. This thumb key will do it automatically for you. (Only **B** is affected by this key. All other notes are unaltered.) First try this scale with all notes tongued. Then try it slurred.
You will hear it played both ways on **Track 33**.

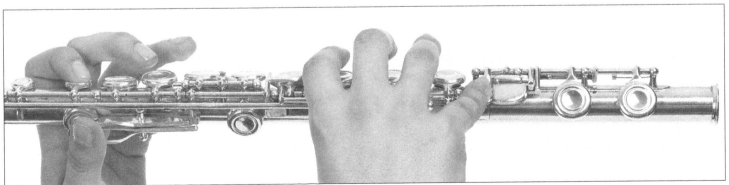

Keys and key signatures

In your head, think of a well-known tune.

Let's use 'Happy Birthday To You' for this experiment. Play the note **D**. Now sing the song starting on the note you just played. *Happy birthday to you, happy birthday to you. Happy b...* and you may find that the note is rather high and uncomfortable for you to sing.

Let's try again. Play the note **G**. Sing the song again, but this time starting on **G**. Easier?

The two versions of the song are in different *keys*. Although the melody is the same, all the notes are lower down.

Listen to the following melodies on **Track 34**. They are the same, but in different keys.

This is in the key of C

This is in the key of F

A melody in the key of **C** will usually contain notes that are all natural. A melody in the key of **F** will usually contain B♭s (with all other notes being natural).

Take a close look at the same melody written out below. Instead of writing the *flat* symbol (♭) before every **B** in the piece, it has been placed at the very beginning of the music, immediately after the *treble clef*. This tells you that you must play *all* Bs as B♭s unless otherwise instructed by a *natural sign* (♮). Therefore it indicates that the piece is likely to be in **F**.

Now play this short melody to get used to playing B♭ if it is indicated by the key signature.

Many styles of music from all around the world involve some form of improvisation. This really means that you make the music up as you go along.

Modern jazz is very complicated and requires a very detailed knowledge of harmony. Some other styles, however, are much simpler and can provide an opportunity to improvise with very little experience of playing an instrument.

Why improvise?

Learning new pieces is vital to improving your ability as a musician, however, music should not just be about reading notes on a page and then practising them until you are fluent enough to be able to perform them. It will still be someone else's creation and will involve considerable time and effort. With improvisation, where there are no notes or rhythms to read, you can just get on with the playing. Close your eyes, focus on how warm and beautiful you can make your tone and 'go with the flow'.

Sunrise

Track 35 is a backing for an improvisation *in the key of* **F** lasting about two minutes. There is no tempo at all for the first minute, so your phrases can be slow and dreamy. Then a slow beat is introduced so you can improvise in a more structured way. Do not play anything too complicated. Leave plenty of rests and only use notes that are in the scale of **F** major, though in any order you like. Remember to use **B♭** instead of **B**: put your thumb on the **B♭** key for the entire piece so you cannot actually play a **B** natural by mistake.

Start the track. Let it play for a few seconds to establish the mood. Now join in, starting on any note you like, playing simple, legato phrases at first. If you happen to play a particularly pleasing phrase, repeat it. Then continue as only your imagination wishes. You can play this piece a thousand times and it will always be different: one of the wonders of improvisation.

Listen to **Track 36** for a demonstration version of this piece.

A piece in the key of F

Here is a piece in the key of F. Plenty to think about here: slurs, dynamics, style, and of course all Bs are really B♭s. (Use thumb B♭ throughout the piece.) There are moments where you need to move smoothly from D to E, so you might like to revise the tricky fingerings for this (see page 28). This piece is in the Classical style of Mozart or Haydn.

You will find a backing on **Track 37** and a demonstration on **Track 38**.

Minuet in F

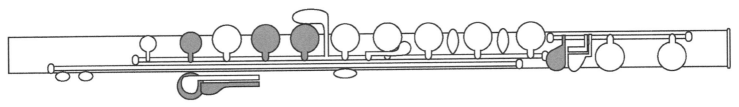

 This note is fingered exactly like the lower **G**, but with the embouchure and airspeed needed for notes of the middle register. You can hear this note on **Track 39**.

Quavers

You have already learnt notes and rests that last for

	4 beats semibreve
	3 beats dotted minim
	2 beats minim
	I beat crotchet

It is time to introduce a note that lasts for just half a beat, the *quaver*. It looks like a crotchet but with a curved tail. The tails of more than one quaver can be joined together to form *beams*.

one quaver and a quaver rest

two quavers add up to one beat

four quavers add up to two beats

Understanding quavers

Although the idea of quavers should seem straight forward, they can be confusing as now you have to start dividing the beats into two. Rather than worrying about the theory, it is better to hear them in action. Here is a fun exercise to help you get used to playing and reading quavers.

The music below is made up of a number of two-bar phrases, all including quavers. On the backing track, each phrase happens twice. The first time it is played for you to listen to how it sounds. All you have to do is repeat what you have heard, just like a call-and-response game.

Set in Stone

Track 40 (1st time **listen** 2nd time **play**)

poco a poco means little by little. The piece starts quietly, gradually gets louder, then fades away little by little.

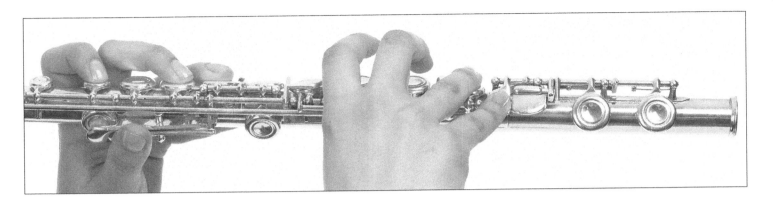

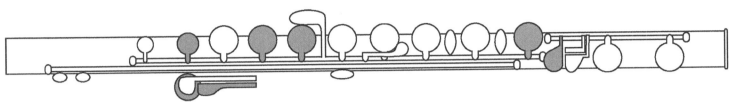

For **F** sharp (**F♯**) you need all three fingers and the thumb of your left hand, and the third and fourth fingers of your right hand.

Just as the flat symbol lowers a note by a semitone, the sharp symbol raises a note by the same amount. This makes **F♯** between **F** and **G**. Listen to **Track 41**. You will hear firstly **F**, then **F♯**, then **G**.

Now that you can play the note **F♯**, you can play the scale of **G** major. You will see the scale written out below, with the **F♯** in the key signature rather than right next to the note itself.

Just as with the scale of **F**, you must practise this often to achieve perfect control.

Concert pieces

Now that you have worked carefully through this book, you should be able to play the pieces on these pages. They are generally longer than your previous ones, and you will have to read the performer's notes as each one may contain a new technique or some notation that you have not seen before.

Practise each one patiently, and you will enjoy performing these pieces again and again.

Performer's notes

Allegretto means just a little quicker than moderate tempo, so this piece should have some life to it.

Every note in this piece should be tongued. Some notes have little dots above them. Do not confuse these dots with dots to the right (note lengthening dots). The ones here mean *staccato*. Play them crisply and slightly shorter than written, but don't play the next note early. (Listen to the demo first to get the idea.)

Spring Antonio Vivaldi (1678-1741). Style: **Italian Baroque**

Track 42 (backing) **Track 43** (demo)

Nepalese Mountain Song

Style: **traditional bamboo flute melody**

Performer's notes

This melody is often heard in the Nepalese Himalayas, played on a simple bamboo flute, although you must aim
to get the richest sound that you can from your sophisticated instrument.

The symbol above the **F** in bars 4, 5, 8 and so on, is called a *mordent*. You play the **F**, very quickly play the **G**, and back to the **F**
(all slurred.) All this should happen within a fraction of a second. You can hear the mordents on the demo track.

Filimiooriooriay
Irish-American. Style: **Irish jig**

Performer's notes

This is quite a long piece. There are only three quavers per bar which implies a quick **1** 2 3 **1** 2 3 feel.
The melody comes in after an introduction of seven bars. The key is **D** minor (which shares its key signature with **F** major),
so you will need to play **B♭**s here, (thumb **B♭** is good). From bar 45, the music is played again, entirely identically except for
one important fact: it is now in **E** minor, so you need **F♯**s, but not **B♭**s any more.
Oh, and one more thing: the note in bar 62 is a high **A** which I will leave you to work out for yourself. It's not hard.
Hold tight and good luck!

By now you should be feeling that you are no longer an absolute beginner. It is a situation you can certainly be proud of. However, there is still a long way to go before you can play one of the Mozart *Flute Concertos*, or the *Flight of the Bumblebee*. So how do you improve from here?

• Find yourself a good teacher. No matter how carefully you read a tutor book, and how hard you practise, nothing is as good as being taught by an experienced player. A teacher will devise a course of study tailor-made to your needs, and will give you feedback on your progress.

• Try preparing for an exam. There are several establishments who can examine students according to a series of grades from I to VIII. This book has guided you some of the way towards grade I. Look at the website of the Associated Board of the Royal Schools of Music (www.abrsm.org) or Trinity Guildhall (www.trinitycollege.co.uk) for details of the syllabus and how to enter.

• Do more practice! The more regularly you practise, the quicker you will improve.

• Buy some flute books. Here are a few you could try to continue your progress:

AM998437 **Really Easy Flute** Favourite Musicals
AM998481 **Really Easy Flute** Favourite Film Songs
AM1000087 **Really Easy Flute** ABBA
AM988350 **Dip In** 100 Graded Flute Solos
AM997909 **Dip In** 50 Graded Film Tunes for Flute
AM995566 **Dip In** 100 Graded Classical Pieces for Flute

Available from all good music stores and www.musicroom.com